The Toolmaker and Other Poems

© David Adès 2025

All rights reserved. Except for appropriate use in a book review, no part of this publication may be reproduced, stored in a retrieval system, or transmitted in any form or by any means, without the prior permission of the publisher, or in the case of photocopying or reprographic copying, a licence from the Copyright Agency of Australia.

The Toolmaker and Other Poems

ISBN 978 1 763825 932

Cover image | Ivan Samkov (Pexels)

Walleah Press
South Launceston
Tasmania, Australia 7249

www.walleahpress.com.au
ralph.wessman@walleahpress.com.au

The Toolmaker and Other Poems

David Adès

Contents

The Toolmaker	1
The Janitor	2
The Bookkeeper	3
The Somnambulist	4
The Poet	5
The Assassin	6
The Mentor	7
The Architect	8
The Barista	9
The Magician	10
The Palaeontologist	11
The Mensch	12
The Storyteller	13
The Tightrope Walker	14
The Clairvoyant	15
The Absquatulator	16
The Invigilator	17
The Locksmith	18
The Fugitive	19
The Survivor	20
The Juggler	21
The Reaper	22
The Catastrophist	23
The Observer	24
The Conjuror	25
The Benefactor	26
The Repairer	27
The Alchemist	28
Acknowledgements	29

Everyone sees what you seem to be, few know what you really are

- Niccolò Machiavelli

About the Author

David Adès is a widely published poet and short story writer with publications in Australia, the U.S., Israel, India, England, Romania and New Zealand. He is the author of *Mapping the World*, *Afloat in Light*, *The Heart's Lush Gardens* and the chapbook *Only the Questions Are Eternal*.

David won the Wirra Wirra Vineyards Short Story Prize 2005. *Mapping the World* was commended for the FAW Anne Elder Award 2008.

David's poems have been read on the Australian radio poetry program Poetica and have also featured on the U.S. radio poetry program Prosody. David's poetry has thrice been nominated for a Pushcart Prize, has won the University of Canberra Vice-Chancellor's International Poetry Prize and has been shortlisted twice for the Newcastle Poetry Prize. His poems have been Highly Commended in the Bruce Dawe National Poetry Prize, a finalist in the Dora and Alexander Raynes Poetry Prize (U.S.) and commended for the Reuben Rose International Poetry Prize (Israel).

The Toolmaker

The toolmaker lavishes attention upon his tools.

So precise, so exact, he sings to them
lullabies and melodies, crooning hymns

and they sing back, a low, deep thrum.

Over the course of a lifetime, he has sharpened his skills —
but humbly, always entertaining doubts,

as if he senses the latent discordant note,

the tool that will fail him and fail to harmonize,
no matter what he tries, no matter how he sings.

When this comes to pass, he keeps the faith:

he knows what he knows and nothing else
and sings the symphony of his loss,

the crashing cymbals of his despair.

The tools answer him, their hairline cracks,
their broken, fissured voices.

The Janitor

The janitor likes to fly under the radar.

Better than a drone, he floats
under the invisibility cloak of bucket and broom,

of mop and wet rags,
noticing every speck of dust, missing nothing.

He is the hidden vault, the repository

of every transgression, every furtive glance,
every swept-under-the-carpet secret.

He holds it all in the avid gleam of his eyes,
in the whisperings of his lips

uttered for no-one but himself.

He is never asked and does not tell,
immersed in the labyrinth of his library,

an infinity of shadow lives,
sad tales, unhappy endings.

The Bookkeeper

The bookkeeper is a serious study.

In pursuit of perfection, she wears seriousness
like perfume: all those pages with dotted i's

and crossed t's, the impeccable script of her hand,

those long white sleeves, that covered skin.
Single-minded, she derives such pleasure

in her pursuit, the tidy ordering of things,

each in its own museum place, the joy,
the relief of balance tingling her soles,

she never sees the ever-mounting casualties

outside the little circle of her light.
The threatening dark is there, to where

she will not raise her sight,

in case it comes for her, entropy's manic
laughter and all things toppled over.

The Somnambulist

The somnambulist keeps stars in the pockets

of his robe, throws his shadow at the moon,
harvests cuts and bruises, a life

kept secret: a double agent

who doesn't know he is a double agent.
He steps into and out of fragments of dreams,

wakes to sleep and wake again,

searching always for something
nebulous as a forgotten memory,

something beyond the periphery, out of reach.

Some mornings he wakes next to a stranger,
in a stranger's bed, where even the mirror

seems to lie, to show a stranger's face.

Slipping into a fog of encrypted days
he wonders if he will ever meet himself again.

The Poet

The poet goes to bed with, awakes in

the warm arms of mystery,
words coming to her like shafts of light,

like drifts of petals, gusts of wind.

She fossicks, excavates,
not for fossils or bones, not for shiny gemstones,

but for other gleamings

she can hold up to the light,
look at this way and that,

not seeking revelation so much as glimpse.

In such fertile ground,
there is so much hidden to be found

the work is endless, the days pass

in a blur between night and night,
mystery's embrace never failing her.

The Assassin

The assassin cannot say when the numbness began,

how it spread so far, what it costs him,
though he knows the genocide of his dreams

was somewhere near the start.

When he manages to sleep
darkness claims him – he no longer dreams.

He does his handiwork focused,

silent as a laser, with no qualm:
not for love or money,

not from rage of distorted ideology,

without passion or revenge.
With him it is more internal:

he kills to push back at the numbness,

to assert himself,
to feel, for a moment, alive.

The Mentor
for Jan Beatty

The mentor is so much more than herself.

She is her own reward:
she is wizard, prospector, pirate, conjurer,

maze of mirrors.

She practices rites of levitation and alchemy,
casts spells, holds students in her thrall.

What treasures come from this cannot be foreseen:

gold leaf on the Buddha,
sparkling raiment, cloudbursts,

citadels of delight. What she begins

takes on a life of its own,
fizzing trajectories of firecrackers

lighting up the dark. She knows

there is no greater reward than this,
her face illuminated in such light.

The Architect

The architect is tired of constraints,

    of pandering to the demands of petulant clients,
economies, utility, function, squeezing more

into available space, the endless variations

and compromises that stunt his designs,
    constrict his breath, give him chest pains.

His dreams are bold, expansive,

    made of air and light, angles, curves,
crisp colors, made of breathtaking beauty

and then he wakes, and all is lost.

He wants a legacy. He wants to build
    The God of Small Things, where every stone,

brick, piece of wood, every tile, every element

    is so finely balanced, in such perfect harmony,
he can walk through a sunlit door, rise, soar.

The Barista

The barista has mastered all the skills of coffee making:

she knows about temperature,
about timing, the art of composition,

the composition of her art.

She knows about aroma and flavour,
how to pour, how to save the world.

She could be anything, and is,

behind the practised movement of her hands,
behind the light coffee chat —

a continent, a rich topography, unfiltered

amongst the coffee bushes
on the verdant earth of Hawaii, Costa Rica,

on the slopes of a volcano in Guatemala,

her dark, her pungent beans, roasted, ground,
the froth of her life only her loves will taste.

The Magician

The magician knows he is no Houdini.

He knows it is not magic he practices
so much as tricks: the tools of his trade

smokes and mirrors, illusions, sleights of hand.

He cannot perfect the perfect trick,
the one he wants the most:

to escape from here and now,

from the trap he has set for himself
with every choice he has made,

the life he cannot leave without leaving

life, the life he cannot lead
without himself becoming illusion.

Somewhere amidst the tricks

he lost faith, believed himself a fraud,
blind to the perfection of the trap.

The Palaeontologist

What draws her in is the lure, the long line,

the slow reel of the past
waiting patiently to be uncovered,

white-boned jigsaw puzzles.

She is patient, meticulous, brushing, sifting,
accumulations of dirt under nails, between toes.

She loves methodology, the absence of speech,

remoteness in which she can hear her pulse,
her breath, in which contemplation flowers.

More than any skeletal find

she uncovers herself, something more
than bare bones, some other history

that is hers alone for the making,

that someone else with patience
and kind hands might one day uncover.

The Mensch

The mensch probes heart, conscience,

finds fault and with it humility,
the need to proffer himself,

to give and give gratuitously

as means to make amends,
in his own eyes at least,

allowing them to raise for a moment

from their downward gaze,
gift returning to the giver.

Knowing fault will never falter,

the proffering is endless,
part of the fabric of the mensch's life,

like breath, rolling in and out,

like remorse, like failure,
like beginning and again beginning.

The Storyteller

The storyteller gives herself to each story,

becomes one with it, absorbing
narrative and characters into herself

until all becomes real in her voice.

She becomes each story she tells,
mesmerizing the children, the audience,

giving them laughter and tears,

giving them faith and belief
until they too become each story.

In her voice, the stories merge

and mingle, braid themselves onto lives,
reach out and draw in,

and those bewitched by her

move as in a trance, the stories
of their lives ripening for the telling.

The Tightrope Walker

The tightrope walker regulates his breath,

hums his mantras, knows his chakras,
seeks balance in all things.

He has practiced and practiced calmness,

learnt to slow his heartbeat,
to empty his mind of errant thought

knowing that each step on the wire

might be his last, that one stumble,
one graceless fall will end it all.

There is no life without risk.

He risks in order to live, and living,
lives in order to risk, always

on some edge, some deep precipice,

embracing the idea of flight, loving
like this too, fearful, exhilarated.

The Clairvoyant

The clairvoyant never explains his gift

nor the burden it imposes upon him,
how he comes to see what he sees,

how flashes of vision, insight, intuition

coalesce into a divining rod to point
in one direction or another.

His art is not science, not forensic,

not often reliable. When he closes
his eyes he sees cloud-mist,

he sees a veil he must lift or pierce,

and beyond the veil a clue, a locket,
a tuft of hair, a red sweater, a map,

a missing child's body, hidden or visible

amongst a jumble of discarded items,
a woman's heartache, a man's bewilderment.

The Absquatulator

The absquatulator is restless as a sea,

seeking the next thing and the next,
breaking wave after breaking wave.

She sits next to exits, keeps watch on doors,

leaves early, looks always to be somewhere else,
thinks life is elsewhere but doesn't know where.

Her aquamarine eyes skid skittishly

past your face, gaze beyond you searching
for another, someone to spirit her away.

She moves from lover to lover,

one after the other slipping through
her fingers, slipping out of her life,

like each promise momentarily held,

each gift, each season, each flickering thought,
each never to be answered question.

The Invigilator

The invigilator prides himself on his keen eye,

his steely attention, paces the room
with measured steps ensuring

that nothing is amiss, that no one

is stealing glances, hiding notes,
trying to slip something by him,

his practiced vigilance. He tries to keep

his thoughts in check, the rampant flight
of desires, fantasies that disturb his peace,

threaten order, but the girl in the third row

in the white blouse has two buttons undone,
the swell of her breast revealing itself

as she leans over, so that passing her he strains

to glimpse an edge of nipple, and she,
looking up suddenly, catches him.

The Locksmith

The locksmith has honed his craft

with patience, guile, a delicate touch,
has become master of his art.

Secretly, he dreams a life of crime,

of silent access to the inaccessible,
a hoard of riches acquired without

a single fingerprint or other telltale sign —

a small indulgence that helps him
as he works, a whistle, a smile on his lips.

He's too devoted to do more than dream,

to stray from his beloved trade,
to let himself drift off into another,

more secret dream, where the alchemy

of his art opens hearts that are locked
to him, that will not yield to his touch.

The Fugitive

The fugitive carries a wardrobe of personas

within her, changing from one to another
as naturally as chameleon: clothes, passports,

hair styles, accents, traversing her selves

like a pack of playing cards so her true self
remains hidden from view

though it stays with her always, substrata,

bedrock from which all else comes.
She studies chess avidly, tactics, strategies,

learning the skill of thinking multiple moves

ahead, how to avoid being cornered,
how to keep her pursuers wrong-footed,

though there is no longer any thrill

in the chase. She knows there is always
an endgame, that she can never escape herself.

The Survivor

The survivor is mother to her brood of wounds,

tends to them gently, is fierce, protective,
never lets them out of her sight.

So much distance travelled from there to here,

so much festering in the wounds she knows
will never heal, but still she croons, she soothes,

she holds them when they weep.

When her sleep is restless, disturbed,
and she wakes bruised and broken

the steel in her rises and she straightens,

she faces another day with fire in her eyes,
defiant, refusing to be bowed or cowed,

shirking nothing. She was not made for this.

What she was made for is gone.
She grieves and makes herself anew.

The Juggler

The juggler had no innate talent or skill:

she learned the hard way, on the job,
by necessity, by way of endless repetition,

first one ball, then two, then three, then four,

her hands a blur of motion, her eyes tracking,
her feet skittering, and always

failure, the dropped ball, the resumption.

It has become habit now, compulsion
as much as requirement,

task overwhelming purpose.

She has no time to remember a time
before juggling, or even to imagine

a cessation of movement, simplicity, leisure.

Such things are forfeit, lost, balls in
parabolic arcs even through her dreams.

The Reaper

The Reaper resents always being described as grim
though he keeps his resentment to himself.

Who would he tell?

He knows it is just one misrepresentation among many
and of lesser consequence than most.

He considers himself more the embodiment of whim,

sharpening his scythe with humour and irony,
approaching his task with the gaiety of fulfillment.

He is a master of levity after all

as the dearly departed rise around him
like a throng of balloons.

It is a wonder they don't hear his chuckle

as he comes to them, his deep *basso profundo*
belly laugh endlessly mistaken for the roll of thunder

after the last lightning strike.

The Catastrophist

The catastrophist is captive to the runaway

train of her anxieties, forever stuck on repeat,
a closed circuit, a never-ending loop

of worst-case scenarios

where nothing can be benign, innocent,
well-intentioned, where alarm bells ring,

danger signs flash, suspicion lurks

in the cloisters of overreaction, blame,
accusation, a never-ending loop

of automatic reflex, of raised voice

and anger, a corralled emotional lexicon,
a distorted vision touching down like a twister

leaving those around to run for cover,

to jump through hoops,
to sift through the debris of its passage.

The Observer

With her keen and restless eye, she tries

to slake her thirst and fails. Image after image
comes to her and she takes them in like orphans,

looking for hidden patterns, until she is faint

and dizzy. She knows that everything seen
changes its behaviour and so becomes

other than itself. In this way, she is always

noticed and nothing is what it seems.
She chides herself, but cannot look away:

there is mystery here for the unpicking

and she is addicted, even if the job is never complete.
Look, the images say, and she looks and sees,

and sometimes she hears a pulse, a rhythm,

a song, and something deep inside her stirs,
something like grace, something like harmony.

The Conjurer

The conjurer works with air, with space,

shaping with body and will
what is not visible, what is hidden,

his hands a craft and the air clay,

not fashioning a golem or trickster
but a sanctuary,

making love from a wish,

happiness from a laugh,
something out of nothing,

out of gesture, attention,

open face and open heart,
small kindnesses, quiet words,

knowing other ways

but turning always back to this,
rewards he both hands out and keeps.

The Benefactor

The benefactor wishes only to pass on what she has received.

She desires to give even when what she gives
is not desired. Her stock is not simply money

or purchases neatly wrapped, but less tangible things,

castles made of air, horizons around her neck,
imagination's limitless bounty,

a gushing sluice of stories from the far reaches

of experience, collective memory, other lives.
Her interest is in letting go, not holding on,

pure to the notion that what comes around, goes around.

Once the gift is given, she does not wait
to see if it is spurned or taken,

nor ponders what becomes of it,

interested only in moving on
to the next gift and the one after that.

The Repairer
for David Mane

The repairer thrums to the puzzle of the world,

no matter that it is insoluble, that there are billions
of pieces he will never touch,

that each of us see only a tiny sliver of the whole.

He forges his path, noticing everything,
giving each moment and each person his full attention,

sending out invisible filaments, linkages, connections,

and does this quietly, drawing people close
to whisper in their ears, smiling, spilling largesse.

He picks up a piece, tries it with another,

and when the pieces fit, as they sometimes do,
that is his reward, his private joy, and he moves

to another piece, untiringly, through the years of his life:

it is only afterwards that we understand what
he has done, how much has been repaired in his wake.

The Alchemist

The alchemist read the tea leaves of her heart,
found her calling early.

The music of transformation swelled within her.
The sciences, yes, chemicals and potions, flasks, beakers,

and the vectors of contagion,
but she was drawn to more than this, to esoterica,

to the human psyche, to swirling seas of emotional vortices,
to intricate mazes of the soul, strategies, chess gambits,

military manoeuvres, the cut and lunge of politics.
Secretly, telling no-one, she made potion after potion,

refining, discarding, pouring the gold of her beauty
and youth into them, the alchemy of her obsession,

an entire life of toil, patient, refusing frustration,
until her final act, her antidotes destroyed,

a triumphant smile on her wizened face,
removing the stopper, kindness flooding the world.

Acknowledgements

I acknowledge the Wallumeda people, the traditional custodians of the unceded land on which I live and write, and pay my respects to their elders, past, present, and emerging.

Many thanks to the editors of the following journals and anthologies in which these poems, sometimes in different versions, first appeared:

Bareknuckle Poet (Australia): "The Toolmaker"
Blue Pepper (Australia): "The Reaper", "The Juggler"
Burning Word Journal (U.S.): "The Mentor"
Eureka Street (Australia): "The Storyteller"
Illya's Honey (U.S.): "The Barista"
Kentucky Review (U.S.): "The Janitor"
Lothlorien Poetry Journal: (England): "The Benefactor"
Live Encounters (Indonesia): "The Alchemist", "The Catastrophist"
Philadelphia Poets Journal (U.S.): "The Survivor"
Pittsburgh Poetry Review (U.S.): "The Palaeontologist"
Poetica (U.S.): "The Mensch"
Red River Review (U.S.): "The Invigilator"
Schuylkill Valley Journal (U.S.): "The Tightrope Walker"
Shot Glass Journal (U.S.): "The Bookkeeper"
Social Alternatives (Australia): "The Somnambulist", "The Absquatulator"
Studio (Australia): "The Conjurer", "The Observer"
Stylus Lit (Australia): "The Magician"
Tamba (Australia): "The Assassin"
The Mozzie (Australia): "The Fugitive"
Uneven Floor (Australia): "The Clairvoyant"
U.S. 1 Worksheets (U.S.): "The Architect"
VerseWrights (U.S.): "The Poet"
Voices Israel (Israel): "The Locksmith", "The Repairer"

www.ingramcontent.com/pod-product-compliance
Lightning Source LLC
Chambersburg PA
CBHW060413080526
44583CB00012B/556